KING AND PARLIAMENT

A SELECTED list of books compiled for the National Book League by H. Stanley Hyland, Fellow of the Library Association and a Senior Library Clerk in the House of Commons Library, with the permission of Colonel the Right Honourable Douglas Clifton Brown, P.C., M.P., Speaker of the House of Commons.

★

CONTENTS

★

Published for the National Book League by the Cambridge University Press
Price One Shilling

INTRODUCTION

'You might as well ask me to build a tree,' said Lord Holland when asked to devise a constitution for Murat's Kingdom of Naples. This book list, *King and Parliament*, has been prepared for those who wish to learn more of the tree which is the British Constitution. It is not by any means a comprehensive bibliography on the Constitution — to be that it would need to be very large indeed — for several important works on constitutional law and history will not be found in it which would be essential to a full treatment of the subject. It is not a comprehensive bibliography at all. Its purpose is, by selected references, to guide British readers, and readers from other countries who are visiting Great Britain, to an understanding of the parts played by the King and by Parliament in the government of our country. It is a select book list on the Crown and those who have worn it, and on Parliament, on the way it has grown, and the way in which it works.

King and Parliament offers, within its own limitations of space, as complete a picture as possible of the Royal House — its dynastic history, its ceremonial and pageantry, and its palaces; against this is set a picture of Parliament — its history, its procedure and its Houses. It is unrealistic if not impossible to study the lives of the Sovereigns without reference to their Parliaments, and, especially since the time of Henry VII, quite valueless to study the development of British Parliamentary democracy without relating it to the Kings and Queens who first controlled it and later were controlled by it. For this reason, it would be wrong to suggest that a reader should begin at the beginning of this list and work through the books in Part I, making his way through the lives of the Kings, before turning to select the works he wishes to read on Parliament in Part II. The works listed in Part I under the dynasties and names of the Sovereigns need to be read along with those in Part II. The history of all but the earliest Kings is the history of Parliaments; the history of Parliaments is largely the history of the Sovereigns. The history of both should be studied together.

Part III of *King and Parliament* consists of books which constantly both emphasize this and make it clear. This last Part, more than any other, is the basis of a bibliography on constitutional history; it is in itself a book list on the King *and* Parliament as well as on the King *in* Parliament. The works in Part III, however, have this in common, that they lay emphasis on the constitutional conflict — and its later and happy resolution — between King and Parliament. Parts I and II of *King and Parliament*, then, complement each other; Part III coalesces the other two. There is unavoidably some overlapping from one section into another because books so rarely bow to the logic of a simple classification; but on the whole the arrangement is reasonable and, it is hoped, helpful. [*See also NBL Note on p. 32*]

PART I

THE KING

The people of England will not ape the fashions they have never tried, nor go back to those they have found mischievous on trial. They look upon the legal hereditary succession of their crown as among their rights, not as among their wrongs: as a benefit, not as a grievance: as a security for their liberty, not as a badge of servitude. They look on the frame of their commonwealth as it stands to be of inestimable value: and they conceive the undisturbed succession of the crown to be a pledge of the stability and perpetuity of all the other members of our constitution.

EDMUND BURKE *Reflections on the Revolution in France 1790*

In this section is a selection of biographies of the Sovereigns of England and Scotland. The works on the English Sovereigns are arranged chronologically in the Dynasties as they succeeded each other, those on the Scottish Sovereigns before the Union of the Crowns are placed together in alphabetical order of the authors' names. This saves a great deal of space. Towards the end of this Part of the list, biographies of Consorts are added after those of the Sovereigns, and, at the end, reference is made to works on the life of H.R.H. the Princess Elizabeth, the Heiress Presumptive to the Throne.

DYNASTIC HISTORY
SOVEREIGNS OF ENGLAND AND SCOTLAND
GENERAL WORKS

Their Genealogy

Most of the political histories of the United Kingdom give genealogical tables of the Sovereigns, but few of them are complete. The two best collections of genealogical tables are the following:

Cambridge Modern History Edited by A. W. Ward and others [Cambridge University Press 1902-1912 13 vols.] *See* Vol. XIII *Genealogical Tables and Lists* [Cambridge University Press 1934 8s 6d]
This volume includes tables of the Houses of Tudor and Stuart, and of the Hanover and the Saxe-Coburg and -Gotha lines.

GEORGE, HEREFORD B. *Genealogical Tables illustrative of Modern History* Edited by J. R. H. Weaver [Oxford University Press 1930]
Has tables of the Saxon line before the Conquest, the line of the Anglo-Danish Kings with the House of Godwine, the line from William the Conqueror to Edward I, the Plantagenet, Tudor, Stuart, Hanover and Saxe-Coburg Houses. For Scotland it gives the descendants of Duncan I down to the accession of the House of Stuart, and that House to the Union of the English and Scottish Crowns. [The sixth edition revised and enlarged]

[3]

POWICKE, F. M. Editor *Handbook of British Chronology* [Royal Historical Society 1939] Gives, amongst other things, lists of the independent rulers of England, Wales, Scotland and the Isle of Man, with explanatory notes. The notes on material available for the listing of English Parliaments should be used with the *Interim Report of the Committee on House of Commons Personnel and Politics. [See p. 19]*

General Works which present Biographies of two or more of the Sovereigns of England

Note: For general histories of the House of Stuart, see *pp.* 12, 13

ARTHUR, GEORGE *Seven Heirs Apparent* [Thornton Butterworth *now* Eyre & Spottiswoode 1937] Lives of the princes who were to become George II, George III, George IV, Edward VII, George V and Edward VIII and of Frederick, Prince of Wales 1707-1751.

BAGSHAWE, FREDERICK G. *History of the Royal Family of England* [Sands 1912]

BIGHAM, CLIVE 2nd Viscount Mersey *The Kings of England 1066-1901* [Murray 1929] The author says in his preface: 'The personal equation may seem to diminish in value as time goes on; but the part which the kings have played is vivid; they have been a real factor in the making of England and they deserve an interest not always accorded them in modern studies of national progress.'

BLACKHAM, ROBERT J. *The Crown and the Kingdom; England's Royal Family* [Low, Marston 1933]

BOLITHO, HECTOR *A Century of British Monarchy* [Longmans, Green 1951 21s Forthcoming: July]
This attractively produced and written history of the Royal Family during the past hundred years is being specially published for the year of the Festival of Britain. In it will be found studies of the lives of the Queens and Kings who have reigned since the middle of the nineteenth century, with emphasis on their family lives and on their personal influence on the British peoples.

COOK, E. THORNTON *Her Majesty. The Romance of the Queens of England 1066-1910* [Murray 1926]

Crown of a Thousand Years; a Collection of Portraits of the Sovereigns of England Historical notes by M. E. Hudson [Harper, Holloway 1948 30s leather; 15s cloth] A collection of short biographies of the Sovereigns of England with 44 portraits in colour, beginning with two portraits of Edward the Confessor [one from a manuscript in the British Museum and the other from the Bayeux Tapestry] and ending with a portrait of King George V.

GOOCH, G. P. *Courts and Cabinets* [Longmans, Green 1944 12s 6d]
The author examines the contemporary descriptions of the Stuart Kings and of William III in Bishop Burnet's *History of my own Time,* those of George II in the *Memoirs* of Lord Hervey and Horace Walpole, and those of George III in Walpole's *Memoirs* and Fanny Burney's *Diaries.*

[4]

HARVEY, JOHN *The Plantagenets 1154-1485* [Batsford 1948 18s]
A spirited and sympathetic history of the House of Plantagenet. The
author himself says 'this book will deal only a little in matters of public
policy and affairs of State, and as much as possible in those smaller but
more precious reminiscences of personality and temperament'. The
book is finely illustrated.

HOLDEN, ANGUS W. E. 3rd Baron Holden *Four Generations of our Royal
Family* [Allen & Unwin 1937 10s]

LANCASTER, OSBERT *Our Sovereigns, from Alfred to Edward VIII 871-1936*
[Murray 1936] There are 55 colour portraits of Kings and Queens.
The short biographies printed alongside the portraits are lightly-written
and very readable.

LINDSAY, PHILIP *Kings of Merry England from Edward the Confessor 1042-
1066 to Richard the Third 1483-1485* [Nicholson & Watson 1936]
Mr. John Harvey who wrote *The Plantagenets* mentions this book as one
of his sources: he speaks of it as 'a book which has done a great deal to
dispel the mummified atmosphere which is so often allowed to shroud
the Middle Ages'.

*The Portrait Book of Our Kings and Queens 1066-1911 done in Commemoration
of the Coronation of Their Majesties King George V and Queen Mary.*
With supplementary notes on the Ceremony. Edited by T. Leman Hare
[Jack *now* Nelson 1911] Contains 39 portraits in colour, most of the
early ones taken from 'engraved portraits' in the British Museum, and
8 plates in colour of the regalia. The engravings were not very success-
fully coloured.

VAN THAL, HERBERT *The Royal Letter Book: being a Collection of Royal Letters
from the Reign of William I to George V* [Cresset Press 1937]

VILLIERS, ELIZABETH *The King Edwards of England* [Melrose 1937]

HOUSE OF NORMANDY 1066-1154

William I 1066-1087

BELLOC, HILAIRE *William the Conqueror* [Davies 1933]

STENTON, F. M. *William the Conqueror and the Rule of the Normans* [Putnam
1908]

William II 1087-1100

WILLIAMSON, HUGH ROSS *The Arrow and the Sword; an Essay in Detection being
an Enquiry into the nature of the Deaths of William Rufus and Thomas
Becket, with some Reflections on the nature of Medieval Heresy* [Faber &
Faber 1947 10s 6d]

HOUSE OF PLANTAGENET 1154-1399

Henry II 1154-1189

SALZMAN, L. F. *Henry II* [Constable 1914]

Richard I 1189-1199

NORGATE, KATE *Richard the Lionheart* [Macmillan 1924]

John 1199-1216

D'AUVERGNE, EDMUND B. *John, King of England; a Modern History* [Grayson 1934]

NORGATE, KATE *John Lackland* [Macmillan 1902]

Henry III 1216-1272

POWICKE, F. M. *King Henry III and the Lord Edward* [Oxford University Press 1947 2 vols. 50s]

Edward I 1272-1307

TOUT, THOMAS F. *Edward I* [Twelve English Statesmen: Macmillan 1903]

Edward II 1307-1327

TOUT, THOMAS F. *The Place of Edward II in English History* [Manchester University Press 1936 21s] The second edition.

Edward III 1327-1377

MACKINNON, J. *The History of Edward III* [Longmans, Green 1900 18s]

Richard II 1377-1399

BIRD, RUTH *The Turbulent London of Richard II* [Longmans, Green 1950 18s] This work, which is not a biography of the King, paints a clear picture of the conditions under which he reigned and was deposed.

STEEL, A. *Richard II* [Cambridge University Press 1941]

HOUSE OF LANCASTER 1399-1461

Henry IV 1399-1413

DAVIES, J. D. GRIFFITH *King Henry IV* [Barker 1935]

Henry V 1413-1422

DAVIES, J. D. GRIFFITH *Henry V* [Barker 1935]

JACOB, E. F. *Henry V and the Invasion of France* [English Universities Press 1947 5s]

KINGSFORD, C. L. *Henry V, the typical Medieval Hero* [Putnam 1923]

KINGSFORD, C. L. Editor *The Life of King Henry V* [Oxford University Press 1911] This is an edition of the first life of the King, written in 1513, by an anonymous author.

LINDSAY, PHILIP *King Henry V; a Chronicle* [Nicholson & Watson 1934]

WYLIE, J. H., and WAUGH, W. T. *The Reign of Henry V* [Cambridge University Press 1914-1929 3 vols. Vol. I *1413-1415*; vol. II *1415-1416*; vol. III *1416-1422* 30s]

HOUSE OF YORK 1461-1485

Edward IV 1461-1483

SCOFIELD, CORA L. *The Life and Reign of Edward the Fourth, King of England and of France and Lord of Ireland* [Longmans, Green 1923 2 vols.]

[6]

Edward V 1483

TANNER, LAWRENCE E., and WRIGHT, WILLIAM *Recent Investigations regarding the Fate of the Princes in the Tower* [Reprinted from *Archaeologia* 1935] *Note*: Edward V was deposed by his uncle who became Richard III: Edward and his brother Richard were the Princes in the Tower.

Richard III 1483-1485

LINDSAY, PHILIP *King Richard III; a Chronicle* [Nicholson & Watson 1933]

HOUSE OF TUDOR 1485-1603

Henry VII 1485-1509

POLLARD, A. F. *The Reign of Henry VII* [Longmans, Green 1913-1914 3 vols.]

TEMPERLEY, GLADYS *Henry VII* [Constable 1914]

Henry VIII 1509-1547

HENRY VIII King of England *Letters* Selected by Muriel St. C. Byrne [Cassell 1936]

HACKETT, FRANCIS *Henry the Eighth* [Cape 1929 15s]

POLLARD, A. F. *Henry VIII* [Longmans, Green 1902 New edition in preparation]

Edward VI 1547-1553

POLLARD, A. F. *England under Protector Somerset* [Kegan Paul 1900]

Mary I 1553-1558

PRESCOTT, H. F. M. *Spanish Tudor; the Life of Bloody Mary* [Constable 1940]

WHITE, BEATRICE *Mary Tudor* [Macmillan 1935]

Elizabeth 1558-1603

ELIZABETH Queen of England *The Letters of Queen Elizabeth* Edited by G. B. Harrison [Cassell 1935]

CHAMBERLIN, F. *The Private Character of Queen Elizabeth* [Lane 1921]

NEALE, J. E. *Queen Elizabeth* [Cape 1934 15s]

STRACHEY, LYTTON *Elizabeth and Essex; a Tragic History* [Chatto & Windus 1928 7s 6d]

HOUSE OF STUART 1603-1714

James I 1603-1625

STEEHOLM, CLARA., and STEEHOLM, HARDY *James I of England; the wisest Fool in Christendom* [Covici, New York; Michael Joseph, London 1938]

WILLIAMS, CHARLES *James I* [Barker 1934 10s 6d]

Charles I 1625-1649

CHARLES I King of England *Letters, Speeches and Proclamations* Edited by Sir C. Petrie [Cassell 1935]

BELLOC, HILAIRE *Charles the First, King of England* [Cassell 1936]

HIGHAM, F. M. G. *Charles I* [Hamish Hamilton 1932]

WILLIAMSON, H. R. *Charles and Cromwell* [Duckworth 1946 10s 6d]

WINGFIELD-STRATFORD, E. C. *Charles, King of England 1600-1649* [Hollis & Carter 1949 18s]

WINGFIELD-STRATFORD, E. C. *King Charles and King Pym 1637-1643* [Hollis & Carter 1949 18s]

WINGFIELD-STRATFORD, E. C. *King Charles the Martyr 1643-1649* [Hollis & Carter 1950 18s]

Note on the Interregnum 1649-1660

Charles I was beheaded on January 30 1649, and eight days later the Kingship was abolished. From February 14 1649 until December 1653, the country was governed by a Council of State. From December 16 1653 until he died on September 3 1658, Oliver Cromwell was Lord Protector. He was succeeded by his son Richard Cromwell, who abdicated the office on May 24 1659.

Charles II, son of Charles I and Henrietta Maria, acceded to the throne on May 29 1660. Before his arrival at Dover, a Proclamation had been read on May 8 which said that the Crown 'by inherent birth-right and lawful and undoubted succession' had fallen to Charles as soon as his father had died. He had already, on February 5 1649, been proclaimed by the Scottish Estates to be King of Great Britain, France and Ireland.

For the lives of the Lord Protectors, see;

CROMWELL, OLIVER Lord Protector *Writings and Speeches of Oliver Cromwell* General Editor W. C. Abbott, assisted by D. C. Crane [Harvard University Press, Cambridge, Mass; Oxford University Press, London 1937-1947 4 vols. Vols. I and II 32s 6d each; vols. III and IV Out of print]

ASHLEY, M. P. *Oliver Cromwell; the Conservative Dictator* [Cape 1937]

BUCHAN, JOHN later 1st Baron Tweedsmuir *Oliver Cromwell* [Hodder & Stoughton 1939 25s]

FIRTH, CHARLES *Oliver Cromwell* [Putnam 1907 15s]

RAMSEY, R. W. *Richard Cromwell* [Longmans, Green 1939]

WEDGWOOD, C. V. *Oliver Cromwell* [Duckworth 1939 4s 6d]

Charles II 1649-1685

CHARLES II King of England *The Letters, Speeches and Declarations of King Charles II* Edited by Arthur Bryant [Cassell 1935]

AIRY, O. *Charles II* [Longmans, Green 1904]

BRYANT, ARTHUR *King Charles II* [Longmans, Green 1931 15s]

DASENT, ARTHUR I. *The Private Life of Charles II* [Cassell 1927]

James II 1685-1688

BELLOC, HILAIRE *James the Second* [Faber & Faber 1928]

HIGHAM, F. M. G. *King James the Second* [Hamish Hamilton 1934]

TURNER, F. C. *James II* [Eyre & Spottiswoode 1948 21s]

William III 1689-1702
Mary II 1689-1694

BOWEN, MARJORIE *The third Mary Stuart, Mary of York, Orange and England: being a Character Study with Memoirs and Letters of Queen Mary II of England 1662-1694* [Lane 1929]

RENIER, G. J. *William of Orange* [Nelson 1939]

WATERSON, N. M. *Mary II Queen of England 1689-1694* [Duke University Press, Durham, N. Carolina; Cambridge University Press, London 1928 19*s*]

Anne 1702-1714

ANNE Queen of England *Letters and Diplomatic Instructions of Queen Anne* Edited by B. C. Brown [Cassell 1935]

CONNELL, NEVILLE *Anne, the last Stuart Monarch* [Thornton Butterworth *now* Eyre & Spottiswoode 1937]

HOPKINSON, M. R. *Anne of England: the Biography of a great Queen* [Constable 1934]

HOUSE OF HANOVER 1714-1901

George I 1714-1727

IMBERT-TERRY, H. M. *A Constitutional King: George I* [Murray 1927 18*s*]

MELVILLE, L. *The first George in Hanover and England* [Pitman 1908 2 vols.]

George II 1727-1760

DAVIES, J. D. G. *A King in Toils* [Lindsay Drummond *now* Benn 1938]

George III 1760-1820

GEORGE III King of England *The Correspondence of King George the Third 1760-1783* Edited by Sir John Fortescue [Macmillan 1927-1928 6 vols.]

GEORGE III King of England *Additions and Corrections to Sir John Fortescue's Edition of the 'Correspondence of King George the Third' Vol. I* by L. B. Namier [Manchester University Press 1937 10*s* 6*d*]

GEORGE III King of England *Letters of King George III* Edited by Bonamy Dobrée [Cassell 1935]

GEORGE III King of England *Letters from George III to Lord Bute 1756-1766* Edited by R. Sidgwick [Macmillan 1939 18*s*]

BOUSTEAD, GUY M. *The Lone Monarch* [Lane 1940]

DAVIES, J. D. G. *George the Third: a Record of a King's Reign* [Nicholson & Watson 1936]

VULLIAMY, C. E. *Royal George: a Study of King George III, his Experiment in Monarchy, his Decline and Retirement, etc.* [Cape 1937]

George IV 1820-1830

GEORGE IV King of England *The Letters of King George IV* Edited by A. Aspinall [Cambridge University Press 1938 3 vols. 84*s*]

CRESTON, DORMER *The Regent and His Daughter* [Eyre & Spottiswoode 1932 16s]

FULFORD, ROGER *George the Fourth* [Duckworth 1935 15*s*]

LESLIE, SHANE *George the Fourth* [Benn 1926]

THOMPSON, GRACE E. *The First Gentleman; a Study of the Regent, afterwards George IV* [Cape 1935]

B   [9]

William IV 1830-1837

MOLLOY, J. F. *The Sailor King: William the Fourth, his Court and his Subjects* [Hutchinson 1903 2 vols.]

THOMPSON, GRACE E. *The Patriot King: the Life of William IV* [Hutchinson 1932]

Victoria 1837-1901

VICTORIA Queen of England *Letters of Queen Victoria 1837-1861* Edited by A. C. Benson and Viscount Esher [Murray 1907 3 vols. 63*s*]

Letters of Queen Victoria 1862-1885 Edited by George Buckle [Murray 1926-1928 3 vols. Vols. I and II 52*s* 6*d*; vol. III 25*s*]

Letters of Queen Victoria 1886-1901 Edited by George Buckle [Murray 1930-1932 3 vols. 25*s* each]

VICTORIA Queen of England *Further Letters: from the Archives of the House of Brandenburg-Prussia* Translated from the German by Mrs. J. Pudney and Lord Sudley Edited by Hector Bolitho [Thornton Butterworth *now* Eyre & Spottiswoode 1938]

VICTORIA Queen of England *Girlhood of Queen Victoria; a Selection from Her Majesty's Diaries 1832-1840* Edited by Viscount Esher [Murray 1912 36*s*]

BENSON, E. F. *Queen Victoria* [Longmans, Green 1935]

BOLITHO, HECTOR *The Reign of Queen Victoria* [Longmans, Green *now* Collins 1948 16*s*]

BOLITHO, HECTOR *Victoria, the Widow, and her Son* [Cobden-Sanderson 1934]

GUEDALLA, PHILIP *The Queen and Mr. Gladstone* [Hodder & Stoughton 1933 2 vols. 25*s*]

This selection of letters written to or by Queen Victoria and Mr. Gladstone is prefaced, as the author points out, 'with a commentary in which the two letter-writers are studied at some length, since both have been to some extent the victims of biographical injustice' and, the author continues, 'an attempt is made to set their correspondence against its full historical background'.

HARDIE, F. M. *The Political Influence of Queen Victoria 1861-1901* [Oxford University Press 1938]

LEE, SIDNEY *Queen Victoria; a Biography* [Murray 1902 10*s* 6*d*]

MARRIOTT, J. A. R. *Queen Victoria and her Ministers* [Murray 1933]

SITWELL, EDITH *Victoria of England* [Faber & Faber 1936 12*s* 6*d*]

STRACHEY, LYTTON *Queen Victoria* [Chatto & Windus 1921 7*s* 6*d*]

Albert, Prince Consort 1819-1861

ALBERT Prince Consort *Letters of the Prince Consort 1831-1861* Selected and edited by Dr. Kurt Jagow Translated by E. T. S. Dugdale [Murray 1938]

BOLITHO, HECTOR *Albert the Good* [Cobden-Sanderson 1932]

BOLITHO, HECTOR *The Prince Consort and his Brother: two hundred new Letters* [Cobden-Sanderson 1933]

FULFORD, ROGER *The Prince Consort* [Macmillan 1949 18s]

HOUSE OF SAXE-COBURG 1901-1910

Edward VII 1901-1910

EDWARD VII King of England *Personal Letters of King Edward VII* Edited by J. P. C. Sewell [Hutchinson 1931]

EDWARD VII King of England *Personal Letters of King Edward VII; together with extracts from the Correspondence of Queen Alexandra, the Duke of Albany, etc.* Edited by J. P. C. Sewell [Hutchinson 1932]

BENSON, E. F. *King Edward VII, an Appreciation* [Longmans, Green 1933]

LEE, SIDNEY *King Edward VII, a Biography* [Macmillan 1925 2 vols.]

MAUROIS, ANDRÉ *King Edward and his Times* [Cassell 1936 6s]

Alexandra, Queen 1844-1925

ARTHUR, GEORGE *Queen Alexandra* [Chapman & Hall 1934]

HOUSE OF WINDSOR 1910-

By Proclamation of June 17 1917 King George V announced the assumption of the name of Windsor by his House and Family.

George V 1910-1936

GEORGE V King of England *The King to his People; the Speeches and Messages of His Majesty King George V delivered between July 1911 and May 1935* [Williams & Norgate 1935]

ARTHUR, GEORGE *King George V. A Sketch of a Good Ruler* [Cape 1929]

BRYANT, ARTHUR *George V* [Davies 1936]

BUCHAN, JOHN *The King's Grace* [Hodder & Stoughton 1935]

CARRINGTON, C. E. *The Life and Reign of King George V 1910-1936* [Cambridge University Press 1936]

GORE, JOHN *King George V; a personal Memoir* [Murray 1941 18s; Albemarle Library: Murray 9s 6d]

HUDSON, ROBERT *A Life of King George V; the People's King* [Collins 1930]

'THE TIMES' *King and People 1910-1935* Reproduced from the Silver Jubilee number of 'The Times' May 3 1935 [The Times Publishing Co. 1935]

Mary, Queen Her Majesty Queen Mary

ARTHUR, GEORGE *Queen Mary* [Thornton Butterworth *now* Eyre & Spottiswoode 1935]

Edward VIII 1936   H.R.H. The Duke of Windsor

BOLITHO, HECTOR *The Life and Reign of King Edward VIII* [Eyre & Spottiswoode 1937]

MACKENZIE, COMPTON *The Windsor Tapestry: being a Study of the Life, Heritage and Abdication of H.R.H. the Duke of Windsor, K.G.* [Rich & Cowan 1938]

George VI 1936—His Majesty The King
Elizabeth, Queen   Her Majesty The Queen
Elizabeth, Princess   Her Royal Highness Princess Elizabeth, Duchess of Edinburgh

ASQUITH, CYNTHIA *Queen Elizabeth: her intimate and authentic Life Story from Childhood up till Today, told with the personal Approval of Her Majesty* [Hutchinson 1937]

BOLITHO, HECTOR *The Life of King George VI* [Eyre & Spottiswoode 1937]

MARSH, E. Editor *Our Royal Family* [Littlebury, Worcester 1949 6s; 2s 6d]

MORRAH, DERMOT *The Royal Family* [King George's Jubilee Trust; Odhams Press 1950 8s 6d]

MORRAH, DERMOT *The Royal Family in Africa* [Hutchinson 1947]

MORRAH, DERMOT *The Royal Family in War-Time* [King George's Jubilee Trust; Odhams Press 1945]

MORRAH, DERMOT *Princess Elizabeth: Duchess of Edinburgh* [King George's Jubilee Trust; Odhams Press 1950]

MORRAH, DERMOT., and SHEW, BETTY *Princess Elizabeth; the Story of Twenty-One Years in the Life of the Heir Presumptive* [Odhams Press 1947]

Our King and Queen: an intimate, authentic and authoritative biography etc. [Hutchinson 1937]

PEACOCK, IRENE *H.R.H. Princess Elizabeth* [Hutchinson 1949 10s 6d]

Royal Album Edited by H. Tatlock-Miller and Loudon Sainthill [Hutchinson 1951 25s Forthcoming: July]

SOVEREIGNS OF SCOTLAND BEFORE THE UNION

BALFOUR-MELVILLE, E. W. M. *James I King of Scots 1406-1437* [Methuen 1934]

COOK, E. THORNTON *Their Majesties of Scotland* [Murray 1928]
The author, says Professor Rait, in his introduction to the work, 'seems to me to have succeeded in combining the national with the personal interest of the theme she has chosen'.

COWAN, SAMUEL *The Royal House of Stuart: from its Origin to the Accession of the House of Hanover* [Greening 1908 2 vols.]

DUNBAR, A. D. *Scottish Kings: a revised Chronology of Scottish History 1005-1625* [Douglas, Edinburgh 1907] The second edition.

FERGUSSON, JAMES *Alexander the Third* [A. MacLehose 1937]

FRANCIS, GRANT R. *Scotland's Royal Line; the tragic House of Stuart* [Murray 1928 21s]

[12]

HENDERSON, T. F. *Mary Queen of Scots, her Environment and Tragedy* [Hutchinson 1905 2 vols.]

HENDERSON, T. F. *The Royal Stuarts* [Blackwood 1914]

LANG, ANDREW *The Mystery of Mary Stuart* [Longmans, Green 1904]

LINKLATER, ERIC *Robert the Bruce* [Davies 1934]

MACKENZIE, AGNES MURE *The Rise of the Stewarts 1329-1513* [Chambers 1938]
From the accession of David II in 1329 to the death of James IV in 1513.

MACKENZIE, AGNES MURE *Robert Bruce, King of Scots* [A. MacLehose 1934]

STAFFORD, H. G. *James VI of Scotland and the Throne of England* [American Historical Association, Washington; Appleton-Century, New York 1940]

BRITISH HERALDRY AND
COURT CEREMONIAL

The scope of this part of the book list is wider than its title. *British Heraldry* has been taken to cover heraldry, armoury, genealogy [for which see also p. 3] flags, seals, decorations and orders, and regalia.

BARRON, OSWALD *The King's Arms* [See Apollo XXV 1937 pp. 240-243]

BOUTELL, C. *Boutell's Manual of Heraldry.* Revised by C. W. Scott-Giles [Warne 1950 42s]

BURKE, JOHN., and BURKE, BERNARD [Founders] *A Genealogical and Heraldic History of the Peerage and Baronetage, the Privy Council and Knightage* Edited by L. G. Pine [Burke's Peerage 1949 £9 9s] The 99th edition.

CAMPBELL, GORDON., and EVANS, I. O. *The Book of Flags* [Oxford University Press 1950 15s]

CLARK, CUMBERLAND *The Flags of Britain, their Origin and History* [Wilding, Shrewsbury 1934]

DAVENPORT, CYRIL *British Heraldry* [Methuen 1921]

Debrett's Heraldry Edited by Arthur G. M. Hesilrige [Odhams Press 1936]

Debrett's Peerage, Baronetage, Knightage and Companionage Edited by C. F. J. Hankinson; Consulting Editor Arthur G. M. Hesilrige [Odhams Press 1951 £6 6s] The 149th edition.

DORLING, E. E. *Leopards of England* [Constable 1913]
Leopards of England is the first of seven short papers on heraldic subjects; it is an account of the Royal Arms and the 'royal beasts in the Arms of the King of England which we who name them are accustomed to speak of as the English Lions'.

FAWCETT, FRANK BURLINGTON *Court Ceremonial and Book of the Court of King George the Sixth: a Handbook of Ceremonial at the Court . . . with all necessary information regarding Royal Functions and Ceremonies* [Gale & Polden 1937 12s 6d]

FELLOWES, EDMUND H. *The Knights of the Garter 1348-1939, with a complete List of the Stall-Plates in St. George's Chapel* [Oxley, Windsor 1939]

[13]

FOX-DAVIES, A. C. *The Book of Public Arms, a complete Encyclopaedia of all Royal, Territorial, Municipal, Corporate, Official and Impersonal Arms* [Jack *now* Nelson 1915]

FOX-DAVIES, A. C. *A Complete Guide to Heraldry* [Nelson 1950 35*s*]

GORDON, W. J., and HOLOHAN, V. W. *A Manual of Flags* [Warne 1933]
A well-illustrated guide to the flags of the world with notes on their history and development.

GRANT, FRANCIS J. *The Manual of Heraldry* [Grant, Edinburgh 1937 6*s*]
A complete manual for the student of heraldry, armoury and genealogy explaining the use of armorial bearings in the study of history.

HOLMES, M. R. *The Crowns of England* [*See Archaeologia* lxxxvi 1937 pp. 73-90]
A history of the Crowns of England from the eleventh century, with six plates.

HOPE, W. H. ST. JOHN *A Grammar of English Heraldry* [Cambridge University Press 1913 3*s* 6*d*]

INNES OF LEARNEY, THOMAS *Scots Heraldry, a Practical Handbook, the Historical Principles and modern application of the Art and Science* [Oliver & Boyd 1934 10*s* 6*d*] A new edition is in preparation.

JENKINSON, HILARY *The Great Seal of England* [*See Archaeologia* lxxxv 1936 pp. 293-340] In the plates — there are sixteen of them — are illustrations of great seals from Henry III to George V.

JOCELYN, A. Editor *The Orders, Decorations and Medals of the World* Vol. I *The British Empire* [Nicholson & Watson 1934]

MACMILLAN, WILLIAM *Scottish Symbols, Royal, National and Ecclesiastical, their History and Heraldic Significance* [Gardner, Paisley 1916]

MACMILLAN, WILLIAM., and STEWART, JOHN A. *The Story of the Scottish Flag* [Hopkins, Glasgow 1925]

MAXWELL-LYTE, H. C. *Historical Notes on the Use of the Great Seal of England* [H.M. Stationery Office 1926]

MEGAW, B. R. S. *Notes on the Manx Flag* [See *Journal of the Manx Museum* v 1941 pp. 47-48]

NAPIER, GEORGE G. *English Heraldry 1215-1930* [Edinburgh 1935]
Genealogical tables, and plates with heraldic descriptions.

PERKINS, J. H. T. *The Most Honourable Order of the Bath* [Faith Press 1920]

PERRIN, W. G. *British Flags: their early History, and their Development at Sea: with an Account of the Origin of the Flag as a National Device* [Cambridge University Press 1923 15*s*]

PUREY-CUST, A. P. *The Collar of SS: a History and a Conjecture* [Richard Jackson, Leeds 1910]

REYNOLDS, E. E. *Introduction to Heraldry* [Methuen 1940 7*s* 6*d*]

LEGGE-BOURKE, E: A. H. *The King's Guards* [Macdonald 1951 25*s* Forthcoming: August]
An illustrated account of the Household Cavalry and the Brigade of Guards. Two shorter works by Major Legge-Bourke are: *The Household Cavalry on Ceremonial Occasions* and *The Brigade of Guards on Ceremonial Occasions* [Macdonald 1951 8*s* 6*d* each Forthcoming]

SAINT ANDREW SOCIETY *The Royal Arms and National Flags* [The Society, Glasgow, n.d.]

SCHRAMM, P. E. *History of the English Coronation* [Oxford University Press 1937 15*s*]

SCOTT-GILES, C. W. *The Romance of Heraldry* [Dent 1951 21*s*]

TILLETT, E. D. *The Royal House of Windsor* [Royal Warrant Holders Association 1937] Thirty-five heraldic illustrations.

TILMAN, G. A. *Dress and Insignia worn at His Majesty's Court* [Harrison 1937 3 parts 25*s* Part I *Full Dress and Levée Dress, including Schedules of Household and Civil Uniforms*; part II *Wearing of Insignia*; part III *Scale of Precedence, Court and Levée Regulations, Undress, Evening Dress, etc.*] The Earl Marshal's and His Majesty's Officers of Arms's dress and insignia are described and illustrated.

Titles and Forms of Address [A. & C. Black 1949 7*s* 6*d*] The seventh edition.

TWINING, E. F. *The English Regalia and Crown Jewels in The Tower of London* [Lapworth 1947 1*s* 6*d*]

TWINING, E. F. *The Scottish Regalia* [Street & Massey 1936]

WAGNER, ANTHONY R. *Heraldry in England* [King Penguin: Penguin Books 1946]

WAGNER, ANTHONY R. *Historic Heraldry of Britain* [Oxford University Press 1939]

WOLLASTON, GERALD W. Heraldry [See *Journal of the Royal Society of Arts* lxxxi 1933 pp. 574-586] A good account of the administration of heraldry in England.

WYON, ALFRED B. *The Great Seals of England from the earliest period to the present time, arranged and illustrated with descriptive and historical notes . . . completed by Allan Wyon* [Elliott Stock 1887]

YOUNGHUSBAND, G. J., and DAVENPORT, C. *The Crown Jewels of England* [Cassell 1919]

ROYAL PALACES

This is a select list of books on some of the Royal Palaces, past and present. Some of them, e.g. Buckingham Palace, are not open to the public and can normally be viewed only from the outside. Others, e.g. Windsor Castle, are open to visitors at certain times. Others, e.g. Whitehall Palace, now exist only in part. H.M. Minister of Works has produced short and cheap Guides to many of these palaces: space does not permit the inclusion of these Guides in this list.

BAILLIE, A. V. *Windsor Castle and the Chapel Royal of St. George* [Dent 1927]

BALDRY, A. L. *Royal Palaces* [Studio 1935] Contains photographs of Royal Palaces in and around London.

BEAVAN, A. H. *Marlborough House and its Occupants, present and past* [White 1896] Marlborough House is the residence of Her Majesty Queen Mary.

BELL, WALTER G. *The Tower of London* [Duckworth 1935]

CARKEET-JAMES, Edward H. *His Majesty's Tower of London* [Staples Press 1950 8s 6d] Colonel Carkeet-James, Resident Governor and Major of His Majesty's Tower, has written a popular and well-illustrated history of the Tower, with accounts of its ceremonies and buildings.

CLAYTON, P. B., and LEFTWICH, B. R. *The Pageant of Tower Hill* [Longmans, Green 1933] Though concerned with Tower Hill and not exclusively with the Tower of London, this book is well worth studying if only for its many admirable pictures of the Tower.

DUGDALE, George S. *Whitehall Through the Centuries* [Phoenix House 1950 18s] Mr. Dugdale, who is at the London Museum, has written a splendid — and most attractively illustrated — account of the history of Whitehall. York Place, a magnificently furnished palace used by Cardinal Wolsey became the property of King Henry VIII in 1529; the King rebuilt it and renamed it Whitehall Palace [the Palace of Westminster nearby was falling into decay at this time]. The story of the Palace of Whitehall until 1698 when it was burnt down is told with a wealth of detail. The Banqueting House, long used as a store cellar, as the records depository of the Lottery Office, and later as a chapel, was handed over to the Royal United Services Institution in 1890. It is still used as a museum and is open to visitors.

FLETCHER, BENTON *Royal Houses near London* [Lane 1930]

GEDDIE, JOHN *The Royal Palaces, Historic Castles and Stately Homes of Great Britain* [Schulze, Edinburgh 1913]

GORING, O. G. *From Goring House to Buckingham Palace* [Nicholson & Watson 1937]

GRAEME, BRUCE *A Century of Buckingham Palace* [Hutchinson 1937]

GRAEME, BRUCE *The Story of Buckingham Palace: an unconventional Study of the Palace from its earliest times, together with some Account of the Anecdotes and vivid Personalities connected with it* [Hutchinson 1928]

GRAEME, BRUCE *The Story of St. James's Palace* [Hutchinson 1929]

GRAEME, BRUCE *The Story of Windsor Castle* [Hutchinson 1937]

HOME, BEATRICE *Royal Palaces of Great Britain* [A. & C. Black 1913]

HOPE, W. H. ST. JOHN *Windsor Castle, an Architectural History* Collected and written by command of Their Majesties Queen Victoria, King Edward VII and King George V [Country Life 1913 2 vols. £6 6s]
The finest of the books on the Castle, splendidly produced and illustrated.

HUSSEY, CHRISTOPHER *Clarence House: the Home of Her Royal Highness the Princess Elizabeth, Duchess of Edinburgh and of His Royal Highness the Duke of Edinburgh, K.G.* [Country Life 1949 21s]
A history of Clarence House with an illustrated description of the principal rooms and their furniture.

JENKINSON, WILBERFORCE *The Royal and Bishops' Palaces in Old London with the Parliament Houses and Courts of Justice and the great Houses of the Nobles and Statesmen* [Society for Promoting Christian Knowledge 1921]

LAW, ERNEST *Hampton Court Gardens Old and New* [Bell 1936]

LAW, ERNEST *The History of Hampton Court Palace* Illustrated with 130 autotypes, etchings, engravings, maps and plans [Bell 1903 3 vols. Vol. I *Tudor Times*; vol. II *Stuart Times*; vol. III *Orange and Guelph Times*]

LAW, ERNEST *Kensington Palace Historically and Critically Described* [Bell 1923]

LAW, ERNEST *A short History of Hampton Court in Tudor and Stuart times to the Death of Charles I* [Bell 1924]

LINDSAY, PHILIP *Hampton Court: a History* [Meridian Books 1948 25s]
A popular history with many anecdotes and good illustrations.

MALCOLM, CHARLES A. *Holyrood* [Duckworth 1937]

PYNE, WILLIAM H. *The History of the Royal Residences of Windsor Castle, St. James's Palace, Carlton House, Kensington Palace, Hampton Court, Buckingham House and Frogmore* Illustrated by one hundred highly finished and coloured engravings etc. [1819 3 vols.]
The engravings are superb — and famous.

SANDS, MOLLIE *The Gardens of Hampton Court: Four Centuries of English History and Gardening* [Evans 1950 21s]
An attractive book with illustrations, some in colour.

SITWELL, OSBERT., and BARTON, MARGARET *Brighton* [Faber & Faber 1948 16s]
Includes the story of the rebuilding of the fantastic pavilion 'a process which, throughout the years, converted it from a late eighteenth century dwelling-house into a miniature Indo-Chinese palace — the most peculiar mirage that ever floated above our northern seas'.

SMITH, H. CLIFFORD *Buckingham Palace: its Furniture, Decoration and History* [Country Life 1937]

WARD, CYRIL *Royal Gardens* [Longmans, Green 1912]
Descriptions of the gardens at Windsor Castle [the Norman Tower garden], Bagshot Park, Hampton Court, Osborne, Marlborough House, Kensington and Holyrood Palaces, Claremont and Sandringham. There are 37 plates, most of them in colour.

WAY, THOMAS., and CHAPMAN, FREDERIC *Ancient Royal Palaces in and near London* [Lane 1942] A collection of lithograph drawings by Thomas Way and of comments by Frederic Chapman on the palaces at Eltham, Greenwich, the Savoy, Whitehall, Westminster, St. James's, Kensington, Kew, Richmond, Hampton Court, and on Crosby Hall, the Tower of London and Windsor Castle.

WHITAKER-WILSON, CECIL *Whitehall Palace* [Muller 1934]

WOODGATE, H. PLUNKET *The Tower of London* [Seeley, Service 1928]

YOUNGHUSBAND, GEORGE *The Tower of London* [Jenkins 1918] Abridged as *A Short History of the Tower of London* [Jenkins 1926]

[17]

PART II
PARLIAMENT

'Parliaments, or general councils, are coeval with the kingdom itself. How those parliaments were constituted and composed, is another question, which has been a matter of great dispute among our learned antiquaries; and particularly, whether the commons were summoned at all: or if summoned, at what period they began to form a distinct assembly.'

SIR WILLIAM BLACKSTONE *Commentaries on the Laws of England* 1765

This is a selection of books on the British Parliaments. [There are no references to articles in periodicals; they would have greatly swollen the list.] 'Parliament' means, of course, both the House of Lords and the House of Commons.

Those who wish to take further their study of Parliament should consult the fine collection of references to books, periodical articles, Parliamentary papers and Parliamentary debates cited as footnotes in the latest edition of 'Erskine May' by Lord Campion and Mr. T. G. B. Cocks, see *p. 25*. They should also see *Parliamentary Affairs*, a quarterly journal published by the Hansard Society of London; the *Official Report* of Debates of Parliament [known as Lords' and Commons' *Hansard*] and, of course, the *Journals* of both Houses. The Debates and the *Journals* are published by H.M. Stationery Office.

PARLIAMENTARY HISTORY

ENGLAND

CLARKE, M. V. *Medieval Representation and Consent: a Study of early Parliaments in England and Ireland, with special reference to the 'Modus tenendi parliamentum'* [Longmans, Green 1936]
The *Modus tenendi parliamentum* [*The Manner of holding Parliaments*] here named was written, it is now thought, during the reign of Edward II [1307-1327]. It must not be confused with *Modus tenendi parliamentum apud anglos* which was the title of a manuscript account of Parliamentary procedure written and circulated, though not published, in 1626 by Henry Elsynge senior who was Clerk of the Parliaments. Henry Elsynge junior, Clerk of the House of Commons, published in 1663 a version of his father's manuscript under the title *Of the Form and Manner of Holding a Parliament in England*. A new and correct edition of Elsynge senior's *Modus* was published in 1768 by Thomas Tyrwhitt as *The Manner of Holding Parliaments in England*.

COOK, H. K. *The Free and Independent: the Trials, Temptations and Triumphs of the Parliamentary Elector* [Allen & Unwin 1949 8s 6d]
A short history of representation in England and Wales.

DASENT, ARTHUR I. *The Speakers of the House of Commons from the earliest Times to the Present Day with a topographical Description of Westminster at various epochs and a brief record of the principal Constitutional Changes during Seven Centuries . . . with Notes on the Illustrations and a Portrait of every Speaker where one is known to exist* [Lane 1911]

'Dasent' is a book of many uses. Its collection of Speakers' portraits is of great value and, as a concise and easily written narrative, it serves as an excellent introduction to a study of British political and constitutional history.

FIRTH, C. H. *The House of Lords during the Civil War* [Longmans, Green 1910] From 1649 until 1660 there was single chamber government in England. The author examines the House of Lords in the half century before its abolition — a period in which it 'took an important, and at moments a decisive, part in the defence of the constitution against the Crown'. The restored House of Lords was of a different kind and had a different function.

GNEIST, RUDOLPH VON *History of the English Parliament, its Growth and Development through a thousand years 800 to 1887* [Clowes 1895] Translated by A. H. Keane. A sound though rather ponderous history from the accession of Egbert to the third Reform Bill of 1885. The fourth edition.

GRAY, HOWARD L. *The Influence of the Commons on early Legislation: a Study of the Fourteenth and Fifteenth Centuries* [Harvard University Press, Cambridge, Mass; Oxford University Press, London 1932 25s Only to order from U.S.A.] A volume in the Harvard Historical Studies. With this should be read D. B. Chrimes's critical examination of Professor Gray's thesis added to Chrimes's *English Constitutional Ideas in the Fifteenth Century* [Cambridge University Press 1936 22s 6d]

History of Parliament [H.M. Stationery Office 1936-1938 2 vols. 40s each In progress; Vol. I *Biographies of the Members of the Commons House 1439-1509* by . . . Josiah C. Wedgwood, D.S.O., M.P., in collaboration with Anne D. Holt; vol. II *Register of the Ministers and of the Members of both Houses 1439-1509*] Issued by the Committee of both Houses charged with the production of the History. The Chancellor of the Exchequer, Mr. Hugh Gaitskell, answered a question put on this work by Lord Winterton on February 20 1951 [see *Commons Debates* Vol. 484 columns 1071-4]. The Chancellor announced that the Trustees of the History of Parliament Trust would be given grants-in-aid to enable them to carry on with their work. The decision was warmly supported both inside and outside the House.

HOUSE OF COMMONS *Interim Report of the Committee on House of Commons Personnel and Politics 1264-1832* [Cmd. 4130 H.M. Stationery Office 1931 2s 6d] This report of the 'Wedgwood Committee' is of very great importance to the student of Parliamentary history. It analyses the material already printed on the listing of Members of Parliament and examines the work needed to be done to cover the ground properly.

ILBERT, COURTENAY P. *Parliament: its History, Constitution and Practice* Edited by Sir Cecil Carr [Home University Library: Oxford University Press 1948 5s] Sir Courtenay Ilbert was Clerk of the House of Commons; Sir Cecil Carr is Counsel to the Speaker.

LAW, WILLIAM *Our Hansard, or the True Mirror of Parliament: a full Account of the Official Reporting of the Debates in the House of Commons* [Pitman 1950 8s 6d] It was not until 1909 that the debates in Parliament were taken down and printed *verbatim*. The author tells how this is now done and gives an outline history — it is an outline only — of the long struggle for the correct reporting of debates in both Chambers.

MCCALLUM, RONALD B., and READMAN, AUSON V. *The British General Election of 1945* [Oxford University Press 1947 18s]
A detailed examination of the election with analyses of candidates and parties. Important in the study of Parliamentary representation. See also the later work by H. G. Nicholas on the 1950 election.

MACDONAGH, M. *The Speaker of the House* [Methuen 1914]
A light history of the office of Mr. Speaker with an easily readable account of some of those who have held it.

MACKENZIE, K. R. *The English Parliament* [Penguin Books 1950 1s 6d]
The author describes his book as 'an attempt to explain how Parliament came to be what it is — the origin of its character in English history'. Eight illustrations show what the Houses looked like at several times between 1523 and 1940. A new edition is in preparation.

MORRIS, H. L. *Parliamentary Franchise Reform in England from 1885 to 1918* [Columbia University Press, New York; Oxford University Press, London 1921 21s Only to order from U.S.A.]
This should be read as a continuation to Seymour's *Electoral Reform etc.* see *p.* 21.

NAMIER, L. B. *The Structure of Politics at the Accession of George III* [Macmillan 1929 2 vols. Reprinting: no date]
An important study of the House of Commons in the eighteenth century.

NEALE, J. E. *The Elizabethan House of Commons* [Cape 1949 18s]
Professor Neale says in his introduction: 'It is at this crucial stage in the history of the House of Commons that our study of its structure and manner of working is placed. Who were the members of Parliament? To what classes of society did they belong? How did they come to be elected? How were elections conducted?' These questions and many others are answered. Professor Neale promises to follow this work with a Parliamentary history of Queen Elizabeth's reign.

PARRY, CHARLES H. *The Parliaments and Councils of England chronologically arranged from the reign of William I to the Revolution in 1688* [Murray 1839]

NICHOLAS, HERBERT G. *The British General Election of 1950* Statistical appendix by D. E. Butler [Macmillan 1951 21s]
Like McCallum and Readman's *British General Election of 1945*, this study was presented by Nuffield College, Oxford. It is an important work.

PASQUET, D. *An Essay on the Origins of the House of Commons* Translated by R. G. D. Laffan [Cambridge University Press 1925]
Dr. Pasquet's essay first appeared in French in 1914. This translation is of a revision of the essay made by Pasquet after the publication of Pollard's *Evolution of Parliament*, in conjunction with which it should be read.

PICKTHORN, KENNETH *Early Tudor Government* [Cambridge University Press 1934 2 vols. Vol. I *Henry VII* 16s; vol. II *Henry VIII* 27s 6d]
Two very important studies of the King and Parliament.

PIKE, L. O. *Constitutional History of the House of Lords* [Macmillan 1894]
This is the only history dealing solely with the House of Lords from its beginnings.

POLLARD, A. F. *The Evolution of Parliament* [Longmans, Green 1926]
A very valuable study of Parliament's development. It is, without doubt, the best of the histories, though it must now be supplemented by more recent papers. These will be found listed in the footnotes to Chapter I of Lord Campion's fifteenth edition of 'Erskine May' [see *p.* 25]. The second edition.

PORRITT, EDWARD., and PORRITT, ANNIE G. *The Unreformed House of Commons; Parliamentary Representation before 1832* [Cambridge University Press 1923 2 vols.] See Vol. I *England and Wales.*
Still the best account of representation before the Reform Bill. An enormous amount of research has produced a work which is as readable as it is authoritative. The second volume is devoted to representation in Scotland and Ireland.

ROSS, J. F. S. *Parliamentary Representation* [Eyre & Spottiswoode 1948 15s]
Much of this work, dealing as it does with electoral reform, falls outside the scope of this reading list. The first part, however, in which the author analyses the personnel of the House of Commons from 1918 to 1948, comes within its scope and is of great interest.

SEYMOUR, C. *Electoral Reform in England and Wales: the Development and Operation of the Parliamentary Franchise 1832-1885* [Yale University Press, New Haven; Oxford University Press, London 1915 20s Only to order from U.S.A.] This study is continued by Morris's *Parliamentary Franchise Reform,* see *p.* 20.

TURBERVILLE, A. S. *The House of Lords in the Eighteenth Century* [Oxford University Press 1927]

TURBERVILLE, A. S. *The House of Lords in the Reign of William III* [Oxford University Press 1913]

SCOTLAND

DICEY, A. V., and RAIT, R. S. *Thoughts on the Union between England and Scotland* [Macmillan 1920] Part I, on the Parliamentary government of Scotland from 1603 to 1707, will be found very valuable.

PAGAN, THEODORA *The Convention of Royal Burghs of Scotland* [Glasgow University Press: privately printed 1926]
Based on the records of the Convention. Professor Rait in his *Parliaments of Scotland* has a chapter on the Convention — a rival of Parliament along with the Privy Council and the General Assembly of the Church. This work complements Rait's standard book.

PORRITT, EDWARD., and PORRITT, ANNIE G. *The Unreformed House of Commons: Parliamentary Representation before 1832* [Cambridge University Press 1903 2 vols.] See Vol. II Part I *Scotland*
This is the shortest account of the Scottish Parliament as a representative House. The amount of material assembled is formidable yet very readable.

RAIT, ROBERT S. *The Parliaments of Scotland* [Jackson, Glasgow 1924 30s]
The standard work. All aspects of the Parliament are studied — its place in Scottish history, its composition, membership and procedure, its methods of debate and financial control and its officers, seat and ceremonies.

TERRY, CHARLES *The Scottish Parliament; its Constitution and Procedure, 1603-1707* With an Appendix of Documents [MacLehose, Glasgow 1905]
The emphasis here is on procedure which is traced in its development over the last century of the Parliament's existence.

IRELAND

BALL, J. T. *Historical Review of the Legislative Systems operative in Ireland from the Invasion of Henry the Second to the Union 1172-1800* [Longmans, Green 1889] A short survey of the Councils and Parliaments of Ireland. The second edition.

MORRES, HERVEY R. 2nd Viscount Mountmorres *The History of the principal Transactions of the Irish Parliament, from the year 1634 to 1666: containing Proceedings of the Lords and Commons during the Administration of the Earl of Strafford, and of the first Duke of Ormond, etc.* [Cadell 1792 2 vols.]

PORRITT, EDWARD., and PORRITT, ANNIE G. *The Unreformed House of Commons: Parliamentary Representation before 1832* [Cambridge University Press 1903 2 vols. See Vol. II Part II *Ireland before the Union*]
'Like the Parliament at Westminster it [the Parliament of Ireland] consisted of an upper and lower chamber, a House of Lords and a House of Commons; and the representative system by which the Irish House of Commons was elected was almost a replica of the electoral system of England before the Reform Act of 1832.' This representation is very closely examined.

The Parliament of Northern Ireland from 1920
Under the Government of Ireland Act of 1920, as amended by the Irish Free State [Consequential Provisions] Act of 1922, a separate Parliament and executive government were set up for Northern Ireland.

QUEKETT, ARTHUR S. *The Constitution of Northern Ireland* [H.M. Stationery Office, Belfast 3 parts Part I 1928 3s 6d; part II 1933 31s 6d; part III 1947 15s] The procedure of the Parliament of Northern Ireland is studied in the third Part; the Parliament's establishment is discussed in the first two Parts.

THE ISLANDS

The Isle of Man and the Channel Islands are part of the British Islands but not of the United Kingdom [see the Interpretation Act of 1889]. They have between them, three legislative assemblies which tend to be overlooked even by Britons when they think of the 'parliaments' of the British Isles. The States of Jersey, the States of Deliberation of Guernsey, and the House of Keys of Man can be studied in an impressive collection of official documents but more easily in the following:

BALLEINE, G. R. *A History of the Island of Jersey* [Staples Press 1950 30s]

EAGLESTONE, A. J. *The Channel Islands under Tudor Government 1485-1642: a study in administrative History* [Guernsey Society; Cambridge University Press 1949 21s]

KINVIG, R. H. *A History of the Isle of Man* [Manx Museum and Ancient Monuments Trustees; University of Liverpool Press 1950 7s 6d]
Published under the auspices of the Tynwald.

MAUGHAM, R. C. F. *The Island of Jersey Today* [W. H. Allen 1950 9s 6d]

Nos Iles: a Symposium on the Channel Islands [Channel Islands Study Group: privately printed 1944]

PARLIAMENTARY PROCEDURE

BOSSOM, A. C. *Our House: an Introduction to Parliamentary Procedure* [People's Universities Press; Barrie 1948 7s 6d] The author, who for twenty years has been a Member of Parliament, has 'endeavoured to give a general outline of Parliament's history, functions and procedure'.

BROWN, W. J. *Everybody's Guide to Parliament* [Allen & Unwin 1946 7s 6d]
The author was a Member of Parliament when he wrote this short guide to a Member's duties.

CAMPION, GILBERT F. M. later 1st Baron Campion *An Introduction to the Procedure of the House of Commons* [Macmillan 1947 18s]
A valuable account of the historical development of Parliamentary procedure with very clear descriptions of the present working of the House. Lord Campion was Clerk of the House of Commons from 1937 to 1948. The second edition.

COCKS, T. G. B. *The Parliament at Westminster* [Edward Arnold 1948 4s]
Written for pupils in secondary schools. It is a very useful introduction to the modern House written by the assistant editor of the new edition of 'Erskine May'.

GORDON, STRATHEARN *Our Parliament* [Hansard Society 1948 8s 6d]
Traces the history of Parliament from the Anglo-Saxon Witenagemot and explains the present-day working of the House of Commons very clearly. The author is now Librarian of the House of Commons. *Our Parliament* has been translated into most of the European languages. [The third edition: the fourth is in preparation.]

HATSELL, JOHN *Precedents of Proceedings in the House of Commons: with observations* [Hansard 1818 4 vols. Vol. I *Privileges of Parliament*; vol. II *Members, Speaker etc.*; vol. III *Lords and Supply*; vol. IV *Conference and Impeachment*] John Hatsell was Clerk of the House of Commons from 1768 to 1796. His *Precedents* were first published in 1781. Charles Abbot was Speaker of the House from 1802 to 1817 and was raised to the Peerage as Baron Colchester on his retirement from the Chair. The *Precedents* are a fascinating collection of great value and interest. [The fourth edition, edited by Charles Abbot, Lord Colchester.]

HERBERT, D. 1st Baron Hemingford *What Parliament is and does; being an Introduction to Parliamentary Government in the United Kingdom* [Cambridge University Press 1948 6s] Lord Hemingford had been Chairman of Ways and Means in the House of Commons.

HOGG, QUINTIN MCG. 2nd Viscount Hailsham *The Purpose of Parliament* [Blandford Press 1946 10s 6d] When Lord Hailsham wrote this account of the House of Commons at work he was himself working in it as Member for the City of Oxford. Of particular interest is his clear comparison between the British parliamentary system and the American and Dominion legislatures.

HOUSE OF COMMONS *Special Report from the Select Committee on Procedure on Public Business together with the Proceedings of the Committee, Minutes of Evidence and Index, 1931* [H.C. 161 H.M. Stationery Office 1930-1931 14s]

HOUSE OF COMMONS *Manual of Procedure in the Public Business* [H.M. Stationery Office 1951 7s 6d] Laid on the Table by Mr. Speaker for the use of Members. The eighth edition.

HOUSE OF COMMONS *Eleventh Report from the Select Committee [90th] on National Expenditure. Session 1943-1944, being the Ninetieth Report in the series of Reports from the Select Committees on National Expenditure originally set up in Session 1939-1940. The Examination of National Expenditure* [H.C. 122 H.M. Stationery Office 1943-1944 4d] Contains a historical account of the examination of expenditure by the House.

HOUSE OF COMMONS *First, Second and Third Reports from the Select Committee on Procedure together with the Proceedings of the Committee, Minutes of Evidence and Indexes 1945 to 1946* [H.C. 9-I, 58-I, 189-I H.M. Stationery Office 1945-1946 3s; 2s; 10s] The Committee was set up in 1945 to consider the procedure in the public business of the House and to report what alterations, if any, were desirable for the more efficient despatch of such business. The reports are of immense importance to the student not only for the ideas discussed and the recommendations made in them but also for the wealth of historical information they contain on Public Bill procedure, questions to Ministers, etc.

HOUSE OF COMMONS *Standing Orders. Part I Public Business; part II Private Business. With Table of Fees and Index 1951* [H.C. 27 H.M. Stationery Office 1951 6s 6d]

HOUSE OF LORDS *Standing Orders of the House of Lords except as to Local and Personal Bills and Judicial Business* [H.L. 28, 133, H.M. Stationery Office 1936 1*s* 3*d*]

HOUSE OF LORDS *Standing Orders of the House of Lords relative to Private Bills, Provisional Order Confirmation Bills, Special Procedure Orders etc. with Appendices and Index* [H.L. 31, 133 H.M. Stationery Office 1945 3*s* 6*d*] With Amendments.

JENNINGS, W. IVOR *Parliament* [Cambridge University Press New edition in preparation] A very important study of the working of Parliament. It is clearly an essential work for any serious student of Parliament.

MAY, THOMAS ERSKINE 1st Baron Farnborough *A Treatise on the Law, Privileges, Proceedings and Usage of Parliament* Edited by Lord Campion and T. G. B. Cocks [Butterworth 1950 84*s*]

The fifteenth edition of this standard work on Parliamentary procedure. Thomas Erskine May wrote his *Practical Treatise on the Law, etc., of Parliament* after having served the Speaker as assistant Librarian of the House of Commons for thirteen years. He later became Clerk of the House, an office which he held until just before he died; he was elevated to the Peerage as Baron Farnborough in the very few weeks between his retirement from the Table and his death.

The value of 'May' was immediately recognized. It has never been officially printed but it is none the less 'official' in its scope and status. It is the supreme secondary authority on the proceedings of Parliament — the *Journals* of both Houses being, of course, the primary authority. Lord Campion, the editor of the fifteenth edition [as he was of the fourteenth] was until recently Clerk of the House of Commons, and Mr. Cocks, the assistant editor, is a Senior Clerk in the House.

REDLICH, JOSEF *The Procedure of the House of Commons; a Study of its History and Present Form* Translated from the German by A. E. Steinthal [Constable 1908 3 vols.] Sir Courtenay Ilbert, Clerk of the House of Commons from 1902 to 1921, wrote of 'Redlich' in the preface to this translation: 'Dr. Redlich gives for the first time a full and complete account of the changes which have taken place in parliamentary procedure since 1832, and a most instructive and interesting narrative it is.' He makes the point, too, in this preface, that May's *Parliamentary Practice* is, as its title conveys, a practical and not essentially a historical treatise. Redlich therefore [with one chapter in Porritt's *Unreformed House* which deals with procedure before 1832] complements 'May'.

WILLIAMS, O. CYPRIAN *The Historical Development of Private Bill Procedure and Standing Orders in the House of Commons* [H.M. Stationery Office 1948-1949 2 vols. 17*s* 6*d* each] Colonel Clifton Brown, Speaker of the House, wrote of this work: 'I therefore wish to express my opinion that this work by Mr. Williams . . . should be published on the ground that it will be very useful for the work of the House of Commons. On the historical side it provides a chapter of parliamentary history which has never yet been written and which will be instructive to historians, students and officials of Dominion and Colonial Parliaments; and the detailed appendices will save much future research on the part of Members, Officers of the House, and practitioners in private business.' The author was a Clerk in the House of Commons for more than forty years.

THE PALACE OF WESTMINSTER

The Palace of Westminster remains a Royal Palace; it is in the custody of the Lord Great Chamberlain, who is a hereditary Officer of State. To this extent, references to works concerning the Palace might well have been placed with those containing descriptions of other Royal Palaces in the first section of this list. The reason for its being considered separately here is that the Royal Palace of Westminster is an embodiment of the ancient relationship between the King and his Parliament. His Majesty has placed the Palace at the disposal of Parliament.

BATTLEY, JOHN *A Visit to the Houses of Parliament* [Westminster City Publishing 1949 10s] An anecdotal tour of the Palace with some splendid photographs.

BRAYLEY, E. W., and BRITTON, J. *The History of the Ancient Palace and late Houses of Parliament at Westminster, etc.* [John Weale 1836]
A fine and scholarly account of the ancient Palace written soon after the disastrous fire which destroyed most of it in 1834. It is well illustrated.

BUTLER, PHILIP *Houses of Parliament* [Lincolns-Prager 1948 9s 6d]
A collection of nineteen photographs of the Palace of Westminster with a short description of the building.

COOPER, IVY M. *The Meeting Places of Parliament in the Ancient Palace of Westminster* [Reprinted from the *Journal of the British Archaeological Association* 1938] A scholarly work of great value.

COOPER, IVY M. *Westminster Hall* [Reprinted from the *Journal of the British Archaeological Association* 1937] A history of the Hall described in great detail.

DUNNICO, HERBERT *Mother of Parliaments* [Macdonald 1951 7s 6d Forthcoming] The author was Deputy Chairman of Ways and Means in the House of Commons from 1922 to 1932. He takes his readers on a tour of the Palace of Westminster whilst he describes the buildings and the ceremonial occasions of Parliament.

EDEN, GUY *The Parliament Book* [Staples Press 1949 7s 6d]
A brightly written account of Parliament, its Houses and its working.

FELL, BRYAN H. *The Houses of Parliament; a short Guide to the Palace of Westminster* Published with the authority of the Lord Great Chamberlain and the Speaker of the House of Commons. Revised by K. R. Mackenzie [Eyre & Spottiswoode 1950 1s 8d]
The fifth edition of the official guide was published on the day on which the House of Commons first met in its new Chamber. The new building is described in detail. It is much more than a description of the Palace; it contains a deal of historical information on the ceremonies of both Houses.

HASTINGS, MAURICE *Parliament House: the Chambers of the House of Commons* [Architectural Press 1950 12s 6d] Dr. Hastings supports the view that the shape of the Royal and Collegiate Chapel of St. Stephen into which the Commons moved in 1547, and which was burned down in 1834, has had much to do with the shape and the procedure of the modern House. The book is superbly illustrated, authoritative on the architecture of the Palace, but in parts inaccurate on procedure.

HOUSE OF COMMONS *Report from the Select Committee on House of Commons [Rebuilding] together with Photographs, Plans and Sections and the Proceedings of the Committee. Minutes of Evidence, Appendices and Index 1944* [H.C. 109, 109-I H.M. Stationery Office 1943-1944 7s 6d; 3s 6d]

LINDSAY, MARTIN *The House of Commons* [Collins 1947 5s] This attractively illustrated book in the Britain-in-Pictures series has useful information on the procedure of the House. The author has been a Member since 1945.

POPE-HENNESSY, JAMES., and WILD, HANS *The Houses of Parliament* [Batsford 1945] Hans Wild's fine photographs of Barry's Palace of Westminster have a lively commentary by J. Pope-Hennessy.

SAUNDERS, HILARY ST. G. *Westminster Hall* [Michael Joseph 1951 21s] During his appointment as Librarian of the House of Commons, Mr. Hilary Saunders assembled a considerable amount of material on the Great Hall of the Palace of Westminster — the scene of so many important events in the history of the British Kings, Parliament and people.

WRIGHT, A., and SMITH, P. *Parliament, Past and Present: a popular and picturesque Account of a thousand years in the Palace of Westminster, the Home of the Mother of Parliaments* [Hutchinson 1902 2 vols.] Popular in its style and anecdote, picturesque in its illustrations — it is packed with them — and in its descriptions of Parliamentary ceremonial, it is all its title claims it to be.

PART III

THE KING IN PARLIAMENT

'There are two kinds of kingdoms of the which that one is a lordship called in Latin dominium regale, and that other is called dominium politicum et regale. And they differ in that the first king may rule his people by such laws as he makes himself. And therefore he may set upon them taxes and other impositions such as he will himself without their assent. The second king may not rule his people by other laws than such as they assent to. And therefore he may set upon them no imposition without their own assent.'

SIR JOHN FORTESCUE *On the Governance of England* c. 1470

As was mentioned in the introduction to this book list, it was never intended that this should be a full bibliography of constitutional history. This part of the list comes nearest to being the bare bones of such a bibliography. It is clear that no idea of the present constitutional position of the Crown can be obtained without a study of the history of the relationship between Crown and Parliament. This justifies the inclusion of the material listed in this section. It will be noticed that there are here no references to collections of constitutional documents; most of the histories cited, however, make frequent reference to such collections.

ADAMS, GEORGE *Constitutional History of England* [Cape 1935 15s]
Though not the most massive, certainly the most readable constitutional history. The second edition, revised by R. L. Schuyler.

ALLEN, C. K. *Law and Orders; an Inquiry into the Nature and Scope of Delegated Legislation and Executive Powers in England* [Stevens 1945 25s]

ANSON, WILLIAM R. *The Law and the Custom of the Constitution* [Oxford University Press 1922-1935 2 vols. Vol. I *Parliament* by Maurice L. Gwyer; vol. II Parts 1 and 2 *The Crown* by A. B. Keith 40s]
An essential work for the student of 'King and Parliament'.

BAGEHOT, WALTER *The English Constitution* [World's Classics No. 330: Oxford University Press 1928 4s 6d]
The standard short work on the nineteenth century constitution. The second edition [1872] contained an introduction by the Earl of Balfour, which is well worth studying.

BALDWIN, JAMES F. *The King's Council in England during the Middle Ages* [Oxford University Press 1913 21s] A study of the origin and development of the Council and its relations with the medieval Parliament.

BRIERS, P. M., and others *Papers on Parliament; a Symposium* [Hansard Society 1949 6s] Short papers: *The Speaker* by P. M. Briers; *A Question in Parliament* by Sir Herbert Williams, M.P.; *The Independent Member* by Harold Nicolson; *The Party System and National Interests* by Lord Samuel, and *Delegated Legislation* by Hugh Molson, M.P.

CAMPION, G. F. M. 1st Baron Campion, and others *British Government since 1918* [Allen & Unwin 1950 16s] In this collection of studies are Lord Campion's *Developments in the Parliamentary System since 1918;* D. N. Chester's *Development of the Cabinet 1914-1949;* W. J. M. Mackenzie's *Structure of Central Administration* and W. A. Robson's *Administrative Law in England 1919-1948.*

CARR, CECIL T. *Concerning English Administrative Law* [Oxford University Press 1941]

CARR, CECIL T. *Delegated Legislation* [Cambridge University Press 1921] Described by Professor W. A. Robson as 'a masterly little book'.

EDWARDS, WILLIAM *Crown, People and Parliament 1760-1935* [Arrowsmith, Bristol 1937] Though rather disjointed, this history serves as a good introduction to a study of the King in Parliament.

EMDEN, C. S. *The People and the Constitution* [Oxford University Press 1933 18s] The author says: 'During the last hundred years the direct participation of the people [he goes to a great deal of trouble to define this word] in politics has developed side by side with and in close connexion with representative democracy.' He then goes on to examine this enlargement of the people's share in government.

EMDEN, C. S. Editor *Selected Speeches on the Constitution* [World's Classics Nos. 479, 480: Oxford University Press 1939 2 vols. 4s 6d each] A collection of very important speeches from a variety of sources.

FITZROY, ALMERIC *The History of the Privy Council* [Murray 1928 21s]

GREAVES, H. R. G. *The British Constitution* [Allen & Unwin 1948 9s 6d] The second edition.

HARRISON, WILFRED *The Government of Britain* [University Library: Hutchinson 1948 7s 6d] A good introduction to the subject.

HASKINS, G. L. *The Growth of English Representative Government* [Pennsylvania University Press, Pa; Oxford University Press, London 1948 14s]

HOUSE OF COMMONS *Report of the Committee on Ministers' Powers* [Cmd. 4060 H.M. Stationery Office 1931-1932 2s 6d] This Committee was set up 'to consider the powers exercised by, or under the direction of [or by persons or bodies appointed specially by] Ministers of the Crown by way of [a] delegated legislation [b] judicial or quasi-judicial decision, and to report what safeguards are desirable or necessary to secure the constitutional principles of the sovereignty of Parliament and the supremacy of law'. It is commonly referred to as the Donoughmore Committee Report.

JENNINGS, W. IVOR *The British Constitution* [Cambridge University Press 1950 12s 6d] The author begins his preface: 'A writer on constitutional problems must deal either with history or with actuality. This book is of the latter variety.

JENNINGS, W. IVOR *Cabinet Government* [Cambridge University Press 1951 15s] The best work — in the opinion of most authorities — on the evolution of the Cabinet System of government.

JOLLIFFE, J. E. A. *The Constitutional History of Medieval England from the English Settlement to 1485* [A. & C. Black 1947 25s] The second edition.

KEIR, DAVID L. *The Constitutional History of Modern Britain 1485-1937* [A. & C. Black 1950 25s] The fourth edition.

KEITH, A. B. *The British Cabinet System 1830-1938* [Stevens 1951 New edition in preparation: September] Has chapters on the Privy Council, the Cabinet and Parliament, the Cabinet and the Crown and the influence of the King on public affairs.

KEITH, A. B. *The Constitution of England from Queen Victoria to George VI* [Macmillan 1940 2 vols.]

LASKI, HAROLD J. *Parliamentary Government in England: a Commentary* [Allen & Unwin 1938 15s] The author carefully emphasized in his preface that this was not a formal description of the working of Parliamentary Government in England. It is in fact an historical analysis of the functions of the two Houses in relation to each other, the Monarchy and the Executive.

MACDONAGH, MICHAEL *The English King; a Study of the Monarchy and the Royal Family, Historical, Constitutional and Social* [Benn 1929] A study of the King's office, the ancestry and dynastic significance of the Royal Family, the Sovereign's constitutional position and the ceremonial of the Court.

MCILWAIN, C. H. *The High Court of Parliament and its Supremacy: an Historical Essay on the Boundaries between Legislation and Adjudication in England* [Yale University Press, New Haven; Oxford University Press, London 1910]

MAITLAND, F. W. *The Constitutional History of England* Edited by H. A. L. Fisher [Cambridge University Press 1950 18s] A posthumously published course of lectures, 1887-1888. Also in his *Collected Papers* [Cambridge University Press 1911 3 vols.]

MARRIOTT, J. A. R. *English Political Institutions; an Introductory Study* [Oxford University Press 1938 8s 6d] A valuable introduction to the working of the British Constitution. An outline history of the two Houses of Parliament and of the Crown are followed by a study of their inter-relationship.

MAY, THOMAS ERSKINE *The Constitutional History of England since the Accession of George III* Edited and continued to 1911 by Francis Holland [Longmans, Green 1912] An important work which pays special attention to the influence of the Crown from 1760 to the end of the nineteenth century, to the development of the two Houses of Parliament, and to their relationship with each other.

MORRISON, HERBERT., and others *Parliamentary Government in Britain: a Symposium* [Hansard Society 1949 6s] Contains: *British Parliamentary Democracy* by Herbert Morrison, M.P.; *The British Parliamentary System* by the Speaker, Colonel Clifton Brown; *The Birth of a Bill: The Making and Form of Bills: the House of Commons from the Chair* by the Chairman of Ways and Means, Major Milner; *Lobby Correspondents* by Guy Eden; *The Member of Parliament and his Constituency* by Sir Herbert Williams, M.P.; *The Privy Council Today* by Herbert Morrison, M.P.; *Parliamentary Institutions and Broadcasting* by Sir William Haley; *Parliament and the Liberty of the Subject* by J. Chuter Ede, M.P., and *The Palace of Westminster* by Sydney D. Bailey.

RAYNER, R. M. *British Democracy: an Introduction to Citizenship* [Longmans, Green 1946 7s 6d] An elementary introduction to British parliamentary democracy.

SMELLIE, K. B. *A Hundred Years of English Government* [Duckworth 1950 25s] A study of the machinery of government from the Reform Bill of 1832. The second edition.

STRONG, C. F. *Parliament and People 1837 to the Present Day* [University of London Press 1942 4s 9d board; 4s 6d limp]

STUBBS, WILLIAM Bishop *The Constitutional History of England; its History and Development* [Oxford University Press 1891-1896 3 vols. 36s] Bishop Stubbs's history of the constitution is still considered the best general account of the medieval institutions.

TANNER, J. R. *English Constitutional Conflicts of the Seventeenth Century 1603-1689* [Cambridge University Press 1928 18s]

TURNER, E. R. *The Cabinet Council of England in the Seventeenth and Eighteenth Centuries 1622-1784* [Johns Hopkins Press, Baltimore; Oxford University Press, London 1930-1932 2 vols. £6]

TURNER, E. R. *The Privy Council of England in the Seventeenth and Eighteenth Centuries 1603-1784* [Johns Hopkins Press, Baltimore; Oxford University Press, London 1927-1928 2 vols. £6]

ACKNOWLEDGMENTS

The National Book League is indebted to Mr. Hyland for his work in the compilation of this Book List.

———

The Royal Arms are reproduced on the cover of *King and Parliament* by gracious permission of His Majesty the King. The National Book League would like to thank the Editor and the Manager of *The Times* (and the artist, Mr. Reynolds Stone) for the use of this engraving of the Royal Arms. The Royal Badge of the Palace of Westminster is reproduced on the cover and title-page of this Book List by kind permission of the Lord Great Chamberlain.

———

The Compiler insists on thanking Miss Joan Stevenson and her staff of the National Book League for their help in the production of this List.

———

[31]

Note: This Book List is not intended to be exhaustive. All prices are net and are subject to alteration; they should be checked with a bookseller before ordering. Some books in this list may not be immediately available on account of the present difficulties of book supplies. In most cases, booksellers will be able to give the latest information from the publishers with regard to books which are reprinting. Where no price is given within the bracket at the end of the main title entry, the book is out of print. A large number of books in this list are regrettably out of print. Books which are out of print should be available from libraries, or possibly second-hand copies may be purchased. All publishers are London firms, except where otherwise stated. Dates quoted after titles of English books are, as far as possible, those of the latest revised editions. It is not possible to give price and availability of foreign books.

If this Book List does not tell you what you want to know, ask your Bookseller, Librarian, or the Book Information Bureau of the National Book League for further information

First Published 1951

Cambridge University Press
London: Bentley House, 200 Euston Road, N.W.1
New York: 51 Madison Avenue, New York 10
Canada: The Macmillan Company of Canada Limited

All Rights Reserved

Second Series; First Edition May 1951   *Price One Shilling*

Published for the National Book League by the Cambridge University Press.
Printed in Great Britain by The Alden Press (Oxford) Ltd.

N.B.L. PUBLICATIONS: A SELECTION

The following N.B.L. publications [published for the National Book League by the Cambridge University Press] will be of especial interest to Festival visitors:

THE CITY OF LONDON   *Compiled by* Raymond Smith, F.L.A., F.S.A., Librarian to the Corporation of London.
This Book List vividly portrays the great pageant of London life through the centuries. Mr. Raymond Smith takes as the basis of his selection of books 'the one square mile' of 'The City'. 1951 *Pp.* 40 1*s.*

N.B.L. READER'S GUIDES

A series of stimulating introductions to popular subjects of reading. Each Guide consists of an essay by an expert followed by an annotated reading list of some hundred titles. The following Reader's Guides will be published in June, 1951: each one shilling net.

THE ENGLISH SCENE	*By* John Betjeman
ENGLISH CATHEDRALS	*By* John Harvey
ENGLISH COUNTRY HOUSES	*By* Ralph Dutton
ENGLISH FURNITURE	*By* R. W. Symonds

www.ingramcontent.com/pod-product-compliance
Ingram Content Group UK Ltd.
Pitfield, Milton Keynes, MK11 3LW, UK
UKHW042149280225
455719UK00001B/228